The
CLOUD FISHER

The
CLOUD FISHER

A few poems by

JOHN SCOTT
BRINKERHOFF

Book Design & Production
Columbus Publishing Lab
www.ColumbusPublishingLab.com

ISBN: 978-1-63337-184-2

Printed in the United States of America
1 3 5 7 9 10 8 6 4 2

For two beloved young ladies

Lily and Sophie

to discover among their books someday

Contents

"…we saw a series of ancient terraces, obviously man made, and their size suggested impressive ruins to be found there. In a place called Chilchos there are said to be mountaintop fortresses. An ancient pre-Inca road leads out of Chilchos into the jungle. No one knows where it goes.

I keep thinking about that road. It leads out of Chilchos. Into the jungle. And no one knows where it goes."

Tim Cahill
"Cahill Among the Ruins in Peru"

THE CLOUD FISHER

Framed by the patio door—

gray clouds as rumpled and smudged

as the underside of sea ice,

and a gusting wind that prophesizes

harshness coming.

The alarms are false for now,

simple warnings to repent

and examine our summer lives.

A glassy black spider toils up high,

legs no thicker than an eyelash

busily weaving and knotting its net

despite the buffeting tides.

It swings, scurries, soars, holds on,

laboring on with heartbreaking resolve.

Why will it not rest—wait for the wind to fall,

wait for the sun to rise on another day?

Perhaps within its sternly governed soul

there is no room for the notion of tomorrow

or trust in the certainty of passages.

There is only the message of this moment,

calling for lines to be cast and strung right now

as they have always been, even in storm.

It was still fussing feverishly as darkness came,

and I drew the drapes for the evening.

In the morning the spider and its work were gone,

carried away by the current.

I looked for it, I honestly did, scanning the eaves,

brushing aside delicately veined magnolia leaves,

peeking under vivid geranium blossoms,

stepping lightly over droplet-beaded grass,

searching for a single perfect creature

amid the perfection of all living things.

OHIO DOG

No one knows exactly what she is.

A vet guessed part Husky, part Samoyed,

this brindle bear with watchful eyes.

She won't lick your hand, but she'll lean on you,

which somehow says more,

like she'll always be there, but not to serve.

She has a way of walking,

head up, alert but unhurried,

as if everything she sees is hers to spend or save.

She hates the summer heat.

Her steps slow to a doomsday plod.

Her head hangs.

Her heart is in the cold.

Icy air sluicing from the northwest

is new blood in her veins.

I watch her closely then, in the seeping chill,

when she turns her muzzle into the wind

and breathes.

There are messages for her there,

sounds and scents she seems to know.

She is transfixed.

I do not speak or move,

believing it important not to disturb

her communion with the breeze.

In the peculiar way of humans,

I pretend to understand each twitch of her ears,

each shift of her brown eyes.

I imagine that she interprets for me

these currents so clear they seem to come

from the frozen stars themselves.

She tells me that I too

spend my hours feeling far away

from a home I've never seen.

November

It must be cold today, he said,

looking through the glass

at frost on the ground

and snowflakes in the air.

Yes, she said. And windy, too,

as leaves bounded down the lane

under rearing twigs and limbs.

Silence. They watched.

At this point a walker passed by.

He looks chilled, he said,

even though he's bundled up.

And wind-burned, she said.

His cheeks are red.

And the walker looked their way,

wondering how anyone could stay inside

on such a magnificent day.

JAMES

I met a kid named James in college more than fifty years ago.

He was a strange one, but we could make each other laugh.

One evening over beer he said, near tears,

"There's always been something wrong with me."

He had never found a way to get along with life,

or learned how to gain favor with people.

He clashed and fought and retreated in despair.

"Same here," I said to cheer him up, and raised my glass.

James didn't return to school the following Fall.

He spent a couple of years trying to do work

for which he wasn't suited, I was told later,

before killing himself with his father's gun.

The temperature was near fifteen degrees this morning

when I walked through a windswept field not far from home

with my dogs, one old and red

and one young and white as the deep snow itself.

We went down to a grove and pond where we always go,

while they sniffled and danced and chased the way they always do.

In that frozen stillness, we could have been the only ones on earth.

Trudging along under an ashen sky cracked by light from the east,

for some reason I saw James's face clearly in my mind,

his lower lip trembling, eyes flooding behind thick lenses,

and I was sorry he missed the joy of this passage,

which might have seemed to him a splendid moment

      in the best of all worlds.

THE TARTAN BALL

Every year before winter sets in,

when the air smells of broken leaves

and overripe apples and rain,

the clans gather in a rented hall

laddered with long covered tables,

the backs of metal folding chairs

lined up against their sides like shields.

An aisle cuts through the center of the room,

as wide and straight as a street,

for the marching bands and dancers.

In they come, the distant sons and daughters

of Campbells, Gordons, Stewarts, Drummonds,

Murrays, only moments removed from day jobs

or houses pleasantly cluttered with pets and toys.

Men wearing argyles, kilts and bonnets,

sgian dubhs snug against their calves,

cart in picnic hampers and bottles of whisky.

Women dressed to dance enter laughing,

cheeks rouged by the sharpening wind,

and set their children free to run.

Scottish blood grows thicker with every lifted glass.

Those who know how read the tartans and say the names—

colors separate but patterns bind, and thus

red embraces green among the Gunns and Mackays.

After welcomes and homecoming prayers,

voices loosen and lift during hurried suppers

while, outside in the dark, mountains rise and swell

under skins of nodding heather and meadow grass,

veined with rivers and muttering streams,

and the long black lakes fill with stars.

At some silent signal given by tradition,

places are cleared and fresh drinks are poured,

and light drains away into golden candleglow.

Music from the old hills comes striding in—

bagpipes drone and skirl, drums clatter and boom,

brogues under snow-white spats stamp in unison

as every heart soars and every face smiles.

Tunes flow from the highlands to the sea,

to 'Scotland the Brave' and 'Amazing Grace,'

melodies eternally bound to the ache of loss.

Then everyone dances. They skip and swirl,

the children too, laughing through reels and waltzes

unchanged from the clachans where they were born,

until no one has breath or energy to go on.

The packing up is next, interrupted sometimes

by embraces, goodbyes, promises made

while shrugging into coats and bundling up the little ones.

In small clusters they push through the doors,

cringing from the smart slap of the cold,

going to cars, going to exits, going apart,

going home to their bedrooms and pajamas and dreamless sleep

in America.

STILL WATERS

There were no signs of violence,

no carelessly scattered coins of blood

or black button above a crimson bib

or feathered twig pointing skyward from her ribs.

She appeared to have just laid down and died, this doe,

in a bower at the edge of the pond,

protected by a concertina of blackberry vines.

A daily walk had taken me there,

a walk my pale bear-dog and I make every day

in rain or snow, daylight or darkness, year after year,

down a lane between empty, rolling fields

to a trail that descends into woods.

The pond is there, at the edge of the trees,

worn smooth as slate by morning mists.

A neighbor lives in a house not far above,

an old man pained at the time by the private suffering

that wraps every living thing like second skin.

He joined dog and me, hands in pockets

and shoulders hunched as if winter had already come.

"I bought some quicklime for it," he said.

"The county won't come and take it away."

This was a job he didn't want to do, I knew,

so I followed him up the hill to his garage,

hefted the bag onto my shoulder and went back down.

I worked my way to her through the brush and brambles

and covered her to the neck, pouring with care,

tucking and smoothing with my boot

until it looked as if a blanket had been settled over her.

The dog and I passed by each day as fall hardened into winter.

Then winter was surprised by spring early one evening,

in damp twilight and announced by a pair of dissenting geese,

to erase the graffiti of animal tracks from the snow.

By May she was gone, melted by time and rain,

bones scattered by the small marrow-eaters and the coyotes

which sometimes appeared at the tree line like puffs of smoke.

The thickets closed up behind a community of cattails.

Milkweed and wild mint and goldenrod wore the shadows

of Silver Maple leaves. The pond might have lied about the day

the doe came to drink and stayed, for no hint of her remained—

whispered reassurances for late in the afternoon

as we walked into the red light of a sun sliding down,

old man, old dog, dragging long shadows behind.

In Retrospect

December is the cruelest month to me

because it brings us to both beginning and end.

April? I disagree.

December darkness more quickly comes

to confront us with cold eternity

before we're safely home.

Cheerful lights blink in the frost

calling out the names and dates and places

of everyone we've lost.

Our voices lift up carols and prayers

seeking salvation, begging forgiveness,

hoping someone is there.

Then we enter our deepest sleep,

to wait for the slow march of light to remember

the appointments it must keep.

Many things are sadder than death:

Fine words that wither and fade

simply for want of breath;

The untaken step, a withheld touch;

turning away from a fleeting joy

because it costs too much;

The wind-tossed blossoms of May;

a hand fumbling in the air for something

that lies too far away.

One Morning

As I draw slowly from covered warmth into cool darkness,

broken red numbers are as usual, but now there are icicles of light

between the shades and the window frames. Awakening thoughts

bumble as if looking for misplaced socks, seeking evidence

of a changed man—one less irascible, more hopeful—

then, finding none, focus on reasons to rise.

Coffee, a long walk, no place to go all seem good enough.

Feet descend carefully to the floor just past the old dog

stretched out there, twitching to a running dream.

In the bathroom, the daily ritual of tooth brushing, face washing,

pulling on clothes left hanging the night before

so as not to wake the patient wife who continues sleeping.

A ghostly oval hovers in the mirror, from which emerge

two sea-blue eyes squinting out from under

unruly white brows.

This must be me.

The dark house speaks in edges, corners,

shapes, textures numbers of steps and temperatures.

The way forward is found through fingertips, backs of hands,

and messages received from underfoot. Joined now by a young dog,

we three thump down the stairs (thirteen) to the lower rooms—

blinds and sheers and a heavy patio door curtain

are opened to murky winter light that quickly flows in

to settle in comfortably on the furniture.

Roll back time and you'll see grandchildren climbing up,

old friends laughing, a woman half-covered with a lap blanket,

hands busy with embroidery for hours as the TV blathers away.

But right now the space is quiet, empty, not sad, though. Expectant.

Retrieving the morning newspaper requires coat, hat, gloves,

and leashing the young dog which comically leaps up and down

under the baleful glare of the old dog. Coffee scents the air.

This must be home.

Outside, cold stings the cheeks, but not as sharply as before.

The dogs hop onto and over the drifts alongside the driveway,

but the sound has softened from the usual crackle and crunch.

I can see where the sun is hiding, but it stays just out of sight,

waiting to surprise us, to suddenly jump out

across the pocked and jumbled snow—"Peek!"

A little later the dogs and I will take our walk down the lane

to a pond and a patchwork of farm fields,

and they will explore and sniff where during the night

the deer and possums and coyotes have been,

just as we do every morning a little before eight o'clock unless rain

is pouring down. But now, strolling back toward the house,

the man pauses and smiles to hear the frantic telegraphy

of a woodpecker for the first time in the new year.

 He is hopeful after all.

This must be spring.

EMERALD COAST

Consider McKee, no longer young,

ambulating in his peculiar way

through the shifting gutter between the dunes and the sea.

He appears to be drunk, but is merely blind—

casual hollows and hummocks trick his limbs

into an endless game of catch and compensate,

like a man surprised by one more step on the stair,

or expecting a step that isn't there.

Or perhaps he stumbles over thoughts

(he does that too), seeking truth with the suspicion of a shaman

from the bones and stones and blistered sticks

crudely raveled into viscous rope by the last high tide.

He stops and stoops, peers and pokes the dark detritus

like a coroner pursuing the telltale anomaly.

Wisdom lies in the runes of woven root.

Revelation fills the empty carapace.

What ragged fragments he collects, he will later weigh

and carefully mount with the pins and buttons of letters

to blue ruled paper, each sheet a box to be consigned

with a lifetime of others to lightless metal shelves.

He has long since forgotten the spells to restore their lives

and rightful places in some greater continuum,

in fact, now doubts he ever knew them at all,

but stubbornly persists in making his rounds.

Consider McKee, his losses mounting,

finding fleeting solace in the counting of others

passing by in colorful coats of optimism,

and signing recognition with one pale golfing hand.

He tallies the creases and caves, blighted hides,

and broken gaits with empty arrogance but is still embraced by the

congregation, their labors done,

who lift wistful eyes to the east, and pray to the sun.

But one other strays, more sacrifice than supplicant,

serenely balanced on the land's feathered edge.

She does not judge the setting of this table; all things

are appropriate, and rest where they should be.

She does not question the order of events, but accepts

that the feeble, parching crab knows more than she.

Nor does she resist, but welcomes the instant unshuttered

to let the wind and light pass through.

She considers McKee, no longer young,

as natural to the composition and cleverly sketched

to mimic the white-capped, rummaging gulls

as the condominiums beyond resemble chests of drawers.

This man, whose life one long ago August

she first joined then later became, belongs here

as much as the sandpipers skittering about on skinny legs,

as earnest and busy and charming as children.

Her discontent is immobility; her fear is sameness,

a life constructed of hours alike and lived in the airless closet

of stoic purpose. Once gone, she trusts no sorcery to bring her back

to the whole moment of her last step, or the new one of her next.

She, too, bends for tokens in the sand — shiny coins of shell

and nuggets tumbled smooth — but these will be quickly spent as gifts nestled into small hands: "Look! Look what I found!"

She touches the ends of earth to take them home.

Then, within the compass of her sight

and without announcement, the sea is remade.

A dark archipelago roils the flotsam of scattered light;

sleek islands rise with a newborn's sheen,

unfurling slender flags of foam,

baring all the mysteries of the world.

She runs to turn him from his preoccupations,

and lets the secret fall from her overturned hand.

"Look!" she cries.

"Dolphins!"

SALVO

I am forever at odds with the sun—

its light fogs my eyes

and its heat raises a rash on my skin.

My feet will scorch within minutes

and I must cover my head with a hat.

Yet every year I return to Salvo,

a windy, sun-heavy place beside a road

that runs beside a sea.

There was nothing to do there, we found,

some forty years ago when the children were new,

except fish and walk the beach to a distant crooked pier

and run to and from the thumping, tugging surf

and hold up bread to lure clouds of gulls at dusk

and play Monopoly when darkness drew down

and hold sun-dusted youngsters into untroubled sleep—

nothing to do but read, and watch the ocean breathe.

There is still nothing to do there, we find,

as we come together each year, the children

now watching children of their own grow in this light,

except fish and walk and swim and tell stories

far into starlit nights. Our lives lie far behind us,

scattered here and there across the mainland,

connected by computers and cellular phones.

But here, for now, we are all joined by touch and sight and sound.

By week's end my skin has rebelled

and the usual murmurs of sympathy come

from those who are by now

as dark and oiled and sleek as seals.

I envy their renewal,

but shrug and sigh and apply the ointments

because every joy has a cost,

and the heaviest price is paid when we say goodbye.

Others are welcome to spend their eternity

with angels and saints,

or languishing in gilded, glowing rooms

or traveling the cosmos as milky light

or finally gazing upon the face of God.

But I will settle for Salvo,

and holding a hand much smaller than my own

as we trudge toward the rising light

on a path between the dunes.

Children at the Pool

This angular pool is pebbled

with little round heads,

its surface fractured and frothed

by flailing limbs and cannonballs:

    "Watch out!"

leaping, legs hugged in skinny arms,

    "Watch out!"

Some circle above,

to a chorus of squeals and shrieks,

hurrying with short, quick steps,

heedless of sunburned backs and cheeks.

    "Watch me!"

shouting through trembling blue lips,

    "Watch me!"

At the edge they turn from us,

facing the light,

and with fearless joy

fall away from fevered life

    fall away

into the cool, enfolding waters

    of mercy.

To My Niece In Her Fiftieth Year

There is no choir here, no trumpets, no angel band.

Just the sea sighing in and out on silver sand.

Dapper plovers mining the ocean's ragged seam

And the pale crabs skimming like spindrift might have seen

A curious sight, had they chanced to glance our way—

Our small group, heads bowed, encircling a shallow grave

Scooped out of the firm grit below the high tide line

In which lay the gray ashes of your brief, bright time.

Such stark evidence of your mortal existence

Serves only to exaggerate the great distance

You've gone away from us—too far, now, to return.

Your absence and what it means is where our thoughts turn.

Ironically, by leaving, you are always here

Seeming close enough to touch, and yet nowhere near,

As if you had transferred to some foreign country

And are too absorbed by the press of your duties

To call or write or visit, causing a bruised ache

That never subsides, but does not make the heart break.

Or we try to put ourselves in your quiet place,

Nestled within the timeless march of moons through space,

Oblivious to the dull mutter of living

That goes on as before, damning and forgiving

In unequal measures. But it's best not to show

Too much favor or fear to what we do not know.

Best to just sit quietly and linger awhile,

Wander amid all that can be recalled, from child

To now, gather it close enough to see and hear—

All the hours and days and years that followed you here.

MISSOURI

My father grew up in Missouri. He was the second son

of a tall Dutch foundry man with piercing blue eyes.

I guess because they lived in a hard part of St. Louis,

they sought out forests and streams whenever they could.

When the family moved to California, Dad married a beautiful girl

and stayed behind.

For years, my son has fished the same river my father did,

only he didn't know it until I gave him a short story

Dad wrote in the early 1940's or maybe before.

The words were hammered into yellowed rag paper

by the steel keys of an old Underwood typewriter

but clearly read, "the Current River."

Dad died a year before Brian was born,

but they both found peace in fly fishing,

slipping deeply into the quiet and mystery

drawn in sweeping silver lines from the brush

of a slender split cane rod—ten o'clock, two o'clock.

Kindred spirits of the water.

Brian drives across a quarter of the country to get there.

He jounces down winding roads far out of cell phone range

and meets friends from around there. They drink good whisky,

laugh at each other's stories, and fish. Now that he knows about his

      grandpa,

I'm sure that somewhere in the stillness among sun-warmed pools

they find each other.

I have pictures of them, taken on backcountry trips.

Dad in a shapeless hat, face in river-reflected light,

smiling widely through a four-day beard.

Brian in a shapeless hat, a fat trout sagging between his hands,

laughing out loud, you can tell. These are happy men.

They even look alike.

After a week, the group packs up gear and canoes

and makes plans for getting together again next year.

One by one, they wave "so long" and drive away.

Brian heads back home to his daughters and his dogs and his job,

following a white splash of headlights across the map

in an age of marvels.

DIRT ROADS

From a car window late one Saturday afternoon

while passing through a tiny North Carolina town,

I saw a magical parade in softening summer light—

a long, snaking line of dancing, singing people

dressed to the nines in brilliant colors, arms raised high,

black faces and ivory smiles ablaze with joy.

As I walked down a dirt road when I was young,

I saw a woman pinning clothes to a sagging line

who seemed to suddenly wilt, her face slack with grief,

desperately looking for something that wasn't there

in the hard yard and breathless heat,

as bereft as a human can be.

Once, as I sat on a motorcycle at a railroad crossing,

I saw a man jump from the crawling train,

a small suitcase in one hand, his washed-out blue shirt

buttoned to the neck under a shapeless jacket,

who looked at me sharply from under a dark hat

before striding off through dry, pale grass.

They were never aware, throughout the mystery of their lives,

that they had been captured and carried away

to some place they would never see

by someone they would never know

who recalled them from time to time,

to study their glorious rapture or despairing stare

or purposeful glance, each plucked from a long gone day—

someone who remembered them,

and wished them well.

TENDED FIRES
(FOR JOHN K. LORD)

First,

a few carefully chosen sticks from the yard,

arranged as thoughtfully as possible

to ignite one another,

then the solitary light set in their midst.

A dozen times it lurched between life and death

before steadying, stretching, eagerly shedding

                 its delicate skin.

Children,

I thought of children as the fire swung from branch to branch

and quickly ran this way and that.

When it strayed, I gathered it back

and felt the heat begin to build at its center.

Its voice deepened.

Its flames grew certain. Its embers glittered

                 with landed stars.

Friends

came and went throughout the evening,

each feeding the blaze. But tended fires burn longest,

so I circled, prodded, shifted, brought the edges in

until there was little left to do.

The moon was high. Other things needed tending now.

I stepped away.

Heat

fades from my face. I cross the pale lawn.

Hours from now, as I darken the lights for sleep,

I will look down from the window

at the ones who stayed, distant shapes bending

to care for that bright island,

satisfied that its strong red heart

warms them.

FOSSIL RECORD

Every now and then

voices we've not heard before

arise from rocks or sand or stagnant bog

many millions of years away

from where they fell silent.

Tooth, tusk and bone bring wonder,

suggesting creatures of improbable construction,

others of fearsome size and weight,

each living its time with ferocity or dumb dispassion;

remnants that murmur from unfathomable ages.

What are they saying?

And these immortal remains

entombed in amber, oil and ice—

they arrive asleep and whole.

Insects, reptiles, feather and fern.

What marvels, because we also see them now,

among us, as ants and frogs and lizards,

scorpions and stately cranes diving the shallows,

spared, for some reason, from the apocalypses

to continue their changeless generations.

We can study them, touch them if we wish.

What do they mean?

The survivors identify the lost,

but, every now and then the lost return,

left to be found in the beds and banks

of desiccated rivers and vanished seas,

or in clusters of disparate relics

suddenly brought together on a far savannah

when grazing herds and their hunters

paused, looked up, turned their heads toward

a flash? A sound? Something.

Fragments, impressions emerge after all this time.

Why have they come?

THE GIRLS IN AUTUMN

The girls are pretending that it's winter

as they grip the sides of a plastic wagon

which bounces over freshly mowed grass

and dogs gallop alongside, barking.

You can see the snow on their reddened faces

and hear the cold ring in their laughter—

"Faster! Faster!"they want to go, over imagined ice and snow.

And their grandfather happily pulls them

around and around the yard,

trotting in his clumsy way, quickly out of breath,

but unwilling to end the game,

pretending that it's summer.

DRESSING SPACE
(PREPARING FOR AN ARTIST'S FAIR)

She has come to transform these chambers,

so accustomed to being a certain way day after day

as sunlight cartwheels across the floors

with the reassuring cadence of a metronome,

trailing music, laughter, and the clatter of dancers

among slender crosses of shadow toppled from the window wells.

Hands on hips, back curved like a fallen curl,

she contemplates order—

this here, that there,

what shall hang, what shall stand

when and where,

dark eyes synchronizing invisible gears of delight.

With a wave of her hand

she causes wooden birds and copper roses,

angels, vases, and colored stones

to fly and alight, shift and settle,

press into huddled flocks on shelves and ledges

until approval lets them rest.

She goes about casting light into dozy corners,

assigning warmth to indifferent walls,

and planing edges with woven folds.

Her certain sorcery

leaves this space startled, awakened,

suddenly separated from memory.

She would deny such powers, of course,

and find the notion amusing.

After all, she has done this before,

caused change before;

she has studied its signs and subtleties,

and knows it is not magic.

Yet the evidence remains

at day's end, week's end, month's end,

left behind under an orange moon,

engraved in the clockwork of custom—

hips, hands, eyes,

angels, vases, and colored stones.

Jack's Maps

The states, I don't know how many,

are overturned one by one

each webbed with orange-traced highways

like pictures of distant lightning—

New York, North Carolina, North Dakota, Ohio.

They are routes taken on a motorcycle,

every one dutifully drawn in the evenings

of days spent in the peculiar estrangement

of having nowhere special to go on a weekday afternoon.

Some were traveled alone,

the rest with jet-haired Winnie behind him,

a schoolteacher for many years his wife,

and for all the years his friend.

To them, now hovering so far above the freeways

that not even the sparks of sunlight striking metal

could have reached them, they were down there still,

in sublime seclusion, skimming earth yet flying

through all the surprises of air—

the crackle and sting of raindrops,

cool splash of shadows within bright heat,

fleeting scents of mown grass, hot tar,

livestock, baking bread, roses—

not infused in the wind but each a breath of its own,

as they passed unnoticed save for a memory of sound,

a drone that came and went as something loosed

among the sullen sameness of cars.

To them, those tracks were moments embedded in amber,

all caught unaware in mid-stride, even then,

as unblemished and palpable as their last drawn breath.

They tried to describe a few, looking up from the maps

into middle distance as if to see them more clearly

against the square window that overlooked their square yard.

Their faces flushed, they completed each other's sentences,

and watched each other laugh. That was the point, of course.

The stories weren't for us, but for themselves,

to reanimate the two young people before the lines were made,

when they were most vivid together and every arriving instant was a discovery. For hours they embraced in this way,

unaware of how late it was getting.

There was one more trip, unmarked,

no motorcycle, no maps, just her ashes,

which he left beside an old schoolhouse

between a sunburned orchard and a clear stream,

a good place just a short walk

from where the road ends.

Imagining An Old Man Who Lives Down the Street

I have nothing but time,

yet all I seem to have time for

is going to where I've already been,

and the company of friends long last seen.

I find the time to scratch in the garden dirt,

digging, mounding, weeding, and watering

to raise up buttons of brilliant color

that cheerfully shiver and bob in the breeze.

On gloomy days, they seem to burn

with their own light.

There is time for the birds, which flit and flutter

to and from feeders dangling here and there.

I pour into the troughs and sprinkle on the ground

what they like to eat—black sunflower seeds,

golden millet, flax and thistle.

Sweet, red water for the hummingbirds.

Late on summer afternoons, there is a little time left

to sit in the shade of the porch

in my scarred old rocking chair

waving hellos and trading how-are-you-todays

with whoever passes by. They are all good people.

Every morning the newspaper is right outside my door.

I love this life, right now, as it is,

a tranquil embrace.

I'm very comfortable waiting here.

Receding light, descending quiet,

that's all I have time for.

Evening is when my visitors come

to awaken our stories.

Remembrance
And Forgetting

1.

Who are they, the ones we forget?

We forget those who do not touch us,
or touched us once, but long ago.
And those legions who pass by on the sidewalks
with faces closed in practiced anonymity.
And those with whom we laughed once upon a time,
but have no relevance to the time around us now.
And those to whose minds or lives or beliefs or failings
we cannot relate, and do not intend to invite any closer.
And those who live so far from us
they no longer intrude on our thoughts.
And those who have changed, or not,
out of cadence with how we have changed, or not.
And those for whom we have little regard,
or bring too little of importance to our days.

I think of these things
when I realize that I have been forgotten.

2.

 "Grandpap goes in and out," the letter read.
"Sometimes when he wakes up he thinks he's back in Pittsburgh."

Seeing edges and corners in milky morning light
in a small room, hot in summer, cold in winter,
that he just sleeps in, that's all.
Hearing outside the ding and rumble of a streetcar,
muttering automobiles, and in the quiet they leave behind
the woodblock clop of a horse's hooves.
"Hey Dickie," "Hey Joe," loud hails or curses from men in caps
who carry lunch pails from the crooks of their arms
as they tramp toward the bones of new buildings
or deep craters within wooden palisades
or the bang and roar of Neville Island.

Downstairs, breakfast would be cooking,
eggs, thick bacon, coffee, his tall, thin young wife busy
and leaning back chattering, smiling toward the table
by the window. Who's there? Who would be there at this hour?
Who would he want to see?
Maybe the youngest brother-in-law, the curly-haired rake,
home from the Navy, joking over his first drink of the day.
Or the older one, the broken-nosed Croatian boxer
with gravel in his laugh. Or maybe the chaplain's assistant,

who watches everyone through eagle's eyes.
Or no one will be there, just Sally. And he'll sit with a flap of sunlight
on his shoulder, read the paper, talk about plans and possibilities and
maybe that's all that needs to happen that day.

"If that's how it is," my wife said, "it might not be so bad."
Because she believes she was happier there
as Sally's little sister when Sally was nice,
was better off, because she was a child and her mother was near.
However, the trouble with madness is that it takes you back
while leaving you here. She might, with her child's hand, open the front
door knowing Sally is in the kitchen,
and her mother is knitting in her wingback chair,
but others would be there instead, hesitant and fearful,
telling her she doesn't live there, she has to go away,
then there would be phone calls and policemen,
no one familiar.

And what of him? He would know, too,
when he awakens, eager to go to breakfast
and see who's there or what the papers have to say,
when he swings his skinny white legs over the bed's edge
and sets long, bony feet on the floor and rises.
He would see himself in the mirror over the dresser,
catch the portrait of his drawn, sallow face, wispy white hair,
confused eyes, and would know. He might even linger,

watch his hand float into the frame to touch his cheek,
putting changes there.

But sometimes we mistake kindness for cruelty.
It may be that this is a process of discovering where we want to be
or not, dropping in here and there among the numberless seconds
of our faithfully archived lives, and one day when the old man rises,
there will be no mirror on the wall and he will follow
the breakfast smells and muted laughter downstairs
and they will be there in the warmth calling him slugabed
and saying he's wasted half the day, good natured joshing
amid a clatter of china and silverware—
and the girl will open the door
and her mother will set down her knitting
and look at her, beaming, with her arms outstretched.
"There you are!"

3.

The chubby-cheeked kid in the photograph is about ten years old.
He's smiling, looking directly at me from under a winter cap.
The trees are bare; fallen leaves cover his shoes.
His father is taking the picture and he likes his father.
There is something in that expression, not arrogance,
confidence perhaps, an assurance of some sort—of love? Safety?
Promise?—that will carry into the next moments at least.

My eyes, now mostly blind, study his. They are clear,
perfectly focused, untroubled, as yet unaware of their weakness.
There is a mischievous amusement in them too,
a look I see from other people once in awhile, a mild accusation.

They say, "You don't remember me, do you?"
And I must answer, "No."

Memory can punish us at 3 a.m.
Or abandon us as we wonder why we came upstairs.
It might clearly recall things that never happened,
or things that did, but not that way.
It can goad us into being better than we are
or changing from what we've been.
It can paint a self-image we loathe or admire
or simply accept as a curious stranger.
But memory can never show us as we really appear,
save for the moments just gone by.
"Your whole life passes before your eyes," people say,
as if that moment finally reveals our actual identity
and puts a total to the measure of our value.
But however forgotten or mistaken, we will see
only what we already know.

Our true lives are played out
among the scattered memories of others.

4.

Years and years ago, there was a boy.

He lived in a little square house beside a dirt road

infrequently traveled and bound on one side

by huge, swaying trees and a white board fence miles long.

Every summer morning he ran in the early quiet

when the shadows lay thin and flat and dew glittered in the grass,

his legs pumping away as if he could run for days,

as if eager to see where he would be when he finally stopped.

I see him now and then,

running still.

I Have Never Believed

I have never believed that, unaided,

something can come from nothing.

(For that matter, from where did nothing come

that could by itself become so magically fruitful?)

Everywhere I look I see grand extravagance.

Every inch of visible and breathable space

teems with disparate complexity,

and each existing thing, from mountains to mayflies,

is invested with its own clock but the same cycle—

to be born, live, diminish and die.

Daylight shows us this.

The seasons tell us this.

I have never believed that the universe

made itself, randomly casting the stately circus

of constellations, galaxies and glittering stones,

then setting them spinning, circling, flying through the lights

in an hypnotic procession of creation and order.

What other fantastic gardens grow out there, or rivers run,

or blinking creatures huddle in their holes?

We share the bloodline of those scattered beaches

because the stars too have their times

to be born and live and fade and vanish.

Midnight shows us this.

The heavens tell us this.

I have never believed that, behind it all

there is not a singular energy—

implacable, unknowable, ungovernable.

There is too much, there are too many brilliant points

to dismiss with the conceit of explanation.

Humbled by that cold vastness,

yet comforted by its embrace,

we conform clusters of light into things we understand—

a fish, a horse, a hunter and his hound.

We see this, hear this,

from the current that hums within us all—

the force that tends the stars.

ON WINTER STREET

*A tribute to the 200th Anniversary of St. Peter's Episcopal Church,
Delaware, Ohio*

Seekers came from the east in slow rivulets—

Tradesmen, soldiers, profiteers, and some were preachers

Carrying God to lands God never left

Amid majestic forests of elm and ash and burr oak

Thousands of years old. They assembled in towns.

They would stay, build, and make these places home.

With God's help, we will.

In our town, then barely nine years old, the founders said,

We need a church of our own where all can gather

For praise, thanksgiving, and forgiveness,

A place to be baptized, marry and say farewell.

With our hands and hearts we will build

A house for the Lord on Winter Street.

With God's help, we will.

Those now long departed raised blue limestone walls,

A slender spire, a courtyard beside a castle tower.

We, the living, come to kneel in its quiet embrace.

On Sunday mornings, a bell tolls the hour.

Above our crimson door we burn a single light,

A star to lead the wanderers in.

With God's help, we will.

"You will always have the poor," the Teacher said.

Thus, the hungry, homeless, and bereft come and go,

Leaving with whatever sustenance we can offer,

While others called to a purposeful life arrive one by one

To carry on the work that never ends.

These are the seasons of St. Peter's, and why we must go on.

With God's help, we will.

We hope to leave an enduring welcome

Through the peace of our touch in this wood,

Through the prayers of our voices in these walls,

Passing on what was passed to us, giving what was given,

From the first grasped hands and risen hymns

Under the sheltering trees.

With God's help, we will.

Two Set Out
(A Wedding Prayer)

Two set out one day

after lingering on the shore for awhile

among well-wishers and wildflowers,

swaying from foot to foot

in a mist of ivory blossoms

while cool currents stirred the leaves above

and promised summer sometime soon.

With the river at their backs

they leaned toward friends whose pressing intimacy,

so clear in craning necks and rattling laughter,

seemed to beg for gifts of affection,

and patiently managed their attentions

to exactly the point beyond which

they would seem afraid to be alone.

Then they turned to the wide water of their voyage

and the simple craft that would carry them both.

It was modestly laden because, at least for now,

they hungered and thirsted as one.

One foot at a time, steadying each other

(or perhaps preventing a change of heart)

they left all they had known behind.

They sat facing their followers

with foolish smiles and fearful eyes

as the current gently tugged them away.

Who knew what they would become,

or what fates this cheerful union

had stirred awake? Did it even matter?

Perhaps the meaning of life is just the moving on.

The boat diminished, and joined others on their way,

all sliding toward the same far, green rounding.

In unison, the two raised hands and waved goodbye, goodbye,

and my heart boiled over with love and grief.

How strange it must have looked to them

to see both their cluster of friends and me, a stranger apart,

all with arms outstretched in warm farewell.

But unlike the rest, I would never see them again,

and so had to cast my blessings much farther,

more fervently, that they might endure beyond the turn,

and into the treacherous chasms ahead,

and on through the miles that pass so swiftly by,

and on and on into deepening afternoon and westward bend,

and on and on and on

to river's end.

CLEANING DAY

How I would like to tidy up my life—

go back to its farthest rooms

and begin moving along, systematically

sweeping up carelessly flung words,

wiping away lies and petulant sulks,

pausing now and then to repair what was broken

     in anger.

Fortunately I would not encounter any indelible stains

from ending or defiling another's life,

no, nothing that couldn't be fixed

with thoughtful attention

or the replacement of something stolen that held

     little value.

How nice to erase the hundred dusty guilts

that sting me awake at 4 a.m.

and throw out the rough, crude pictures

that now cause me to avert my eyes.

How pleasant it would be to gaze

into darkness and see nothing

       but stars.

Unfinished tasks would finally be done

and unfulfilled commitments honored at last.

Each misjudgment would be reconsidered,

every listless effort left gleaming with zeal.

I would freshen the air with pleasantries,

scent my path with pure intentions and the essence

       of forgiveness.

But, when all is said and done,

and twilight comes to stay,

what would there be to say?

"Oh, what a splendid house. so beautifully kept.

See how orderly it is. so clean, so neat,

yet so profoundly sad, because it looks as if

       no one has lived here at all."

One Evening in Late July

Her voice quavers just a little:

"We took them there so many times,

so many years, as they grew up. Every July.

All of us together.

Now they take their children and grandchildren

but never invite us."

She wipes her hands on her apron

as she removes it, carefully folds it,

and goes out to water the flowers.

THE MEANING OF LIFE

You asked why are we here,

what is our purpose on earth,

that being an all-inclusive "we"

and a comfortably embracing "our."

Is it our calling to help our fellows,

to make their beds and set their tables

because the only way to touch salvation

is by extending our hands?

Or is it our nature to prevail,

to achieve the highest ground,

moral and intellectual and material,

indulging in accumulation to set a standard for all?

Perhaps we are to ignore life altogether

and follow the lure of spiritual clarity,

tirelessly seeking our place among all things,

until we see our reflection in the mirror of heaven.

Sometimes I pretend to be smart enough to know,

and other times play dumb because it's simpler.

But I promise you this—if I discover the answer

I will gladly give it to you, free of charge.

THIS LIGHT

I can't see hardly anything in this light.

I know it's here somewhere.

It just won't show itself.

My mother had a game she played

when we children searched for our Easter baskets.

"Warm, warm," she would smile. "You're getting warmer."

There's no one to say that now.

I'm tired. I'll look some more tomorrow.

It's been missing for so long

another day won't matter.

TRAVELERS

First, we suffer the discomforts of confinement,

retreating into frowning, fitful sleep

to escape the soft pressures binding our limbs,

dogged by dull aches relieved

only by shifting from hip to hip with fetal kicks

while the darkness drones on and on, a rasp on the nerves.

With every yawn and sigh we fight to breathe.

Next we are expelled, unsteady and confused,

into a rushing slop of humanity,

set adrift to divine the meaning of symbols and signs,

and reorder the world from the repetition of words,

aware that our awkwardness both damns and saves us.

as we stumble toward reconciliation.

Alone, we moan from the sheer effort of it all.

We strain to understand and be understood,

and bow to impatience with apologies before moving on,

grope for attachments, however tenuous, in the familiar,

always aware that we will never belong.

We find comfort in worn wood and stone

and vaults of golden air,

but feel our wonder tinged with a longing to leave.

Eventually our days of reckoning come,

of discovering that the sums of experience never balance.

The things we study prove ephemeral,

but what we merely glimpse endures, bidden to mind

by a bruised twilight, a song, the scent of rain,

like seers summoned to help explain us to ourselves

in our time as perfect strangers.

FIFTY BLINKS OF AN EYE
(PLAYING OUTSIDE)

SPRING

streams tumble and froth,
eager to escape the snow.
everything hurries.

at work before dawn,
spider casts its silver net
to capture the sun

with one day to live,
mayflies spread their wings and soar;
it is we who weep

bright flowers, small birds
sharing a hanging basket—
two nests in the breeze

to welcome the spring
daffodils raise their trumpets
but no sound comes out.

dark clouds flying past
crackle and snap in the wind—
the pennants of spring

outside my window
a mourning dove softly moans
for its dear lost stars

fog, like memory,
will sometimes hide what we know
to make a new world

moths play in the light
white flurries on warm spring nights
imitating snow

crowded with colors,
a sloping meadow shows off
its tray of flowers

SUMMER

thunderstorms stalk by,
breathing cool wind, sowing rain,
then go grumbling home

hear the leaves whisper
as perfumed breezes pass by—
summer gossipers

under the hot sun
ribbons of precious water
turn to molten gold

cows in a fenced field,
brown and white nestled in green—
new shoes in a box

the trees fill with leaves,
then hiss and sway in the wind
like tethered balloons

the sun's heavy hand
silences trees, birds, and fields.
the wind holds its breath

the pelican dives,
sharp beak drills into the sea,
mining for silver

the sea grows quiet
when the sun crosses the dunes
on its way back home

chipmunks in the grass
dart among watermelons
made of morning dew

after cruel heat
light, cool breezes come dancing.
such kindness brings tears

silver maple branch
sneaks slyly over the path
to tickle a pond

we lie in the grass
seeing in the summer clouds
the toys of childhood

FALL

as gray clouds gather,
the fleeing geese reveal
how much we have lost

crimson tupelo—
the year's last light left burning
beside winter's door

leaves like golden coins
shimmer and fly in the wind,
leaving the tree poor

the cool breeze, busy
with Indian Paintbrushes,
colors a sunset

silent harvest moon,
pausing above a still pond,
admires its pale face

a doe in the field
is nearly invisible
in matching brown coat

leaves curled into cups
carry raindrops to the ground,
afraid they might break

rabbit darts and stops,
spending these cool autumn days
playing hide and seek

autumn's first cold wind
hurries summer's warmth away,
and the leaves shiver

light fades early now.

cold crouches in the shadows.

the bees hurry home

a cold autumn wind

scrapes flakes of rust from the trees

as it sands them bare

the heart breaks to see

frail autumn go shuffling by

in summer's old clothes

the raindrops are cold.

they tap on the window glass,

asking to come in

two bluebirds flew down

the day before winter came

just to say goodbye

WINTER

when the north wind comes

the pond covers fish and frog

with a silver roof

the deceit of snow—
water hurries, herding stones
beneath what seems still

winter's steely stars
glide along their prescribed paths…
clockworks of heaven.

under a cold sun
leaves wither, fall, and reveal
the bones of the sky

the stream is quiet
as it passes through the field,
letting the snow sleep

the wind sends snowflakes
to remind the fat black bear
that it's time for bed

snow falls soft and deep
over plain and mountainside,
torrents in disguise

in the white moonlight
an old dog sleeps in new snow,
spring left far behind

the trees have grown thin.
light, with no leaves to catch it,
falls straight to the ground

melancholy light,
skeletons of trees in snow—
we search for spring's face

cold wind grips the tree
trying to shake loose one leaf
reluctant to go

cold winter sunlight
resting on the furniture
inside, where it's warm

a cardinal darts
from the heart of a pine tree
as startling as blood

as melting snow feeds
the next green rising we sense
everlasting life

    we turn, turn again,
    faces following the sun
    through all our seasons

WHERE THE GHOSTS GATHER

Cigarette ashes fill the trays

Overheard voices trail away

There is a place, they seem to say,

Where the ghosts gather every day

We stumble down our chosen ways

Pretending work means more than play

While one by one friends drift astray

Where the ghosts gather every day

When we awaken from our daze

More have gone than remain today

They will love us again, we pray

Where the ghosts gather every day.

We linger in lengthening rays

Proposing toasts to come what may

As longer and longer we stay

Where the ghosts gather every day.

READER

Our house was full of books.

I'd touch the vertebrae

of their colorful spines

and then judge by their looks

just what each might have to say.

I loved the feel of them

either opened or closed.

When I followed their lines

they led to buried gems,

and brave dogs, and talking crows.

Later they led to wars,

on earth and up in space,

the gravity of blood

meaning no less or more

than saving our human race.

I joined the Viking hordes,

commanded bombing runs,

and witnessed Noah's flood.

I freed a stone-bound sword,

and fell to earth from the sun.

The lines led far away

from the stout wooden seat

Father tied in a tree.

where I passed summer days,

with the world below my feet.

Meanwhile, I wrote my own

adventure tales and rhymes;

leaning on mimicry

to build planets and towns

where heroes faced evil times.

I dreamt a life in books

among transcendent peers—

trading thoughts on a boat

in the Keys, or "our" nook

in a bar we'd known for years.

I saw myself in Rome

or in a London flat

or perhaps crafting notes

at a table in some

smoky pub where Joyce once sat.

None of it came to be.

Words led to growing firms

and writing staffs instead.

In time I came to see

that life sets all its own terms,

because this story's quirk

proved my luckiest one—

here at day's end I've read

far more and better work

than I ever could have done.

Also by the author:

All In Time

Dinosaurs

www.ingramcontent.com/pod-product-compliance
Lightning Source LLC
Chambersburg PA
CBHW032050040426
42449CB00007B/1049